Astral
Projection
Made Easy

and overcoming the fear of death

Astral Projection Made Easy

and overcoming the fear of death

Stephanie Sorrell

BOOKS

Winchester, UK
Washington, USA

First published by Sixth Books, 2012
Sixth Books is an imprint of John Hunt Publishing Ltd., Laurel House, Station Approach,
Alresford, Hants, SO24 9JH, UK
office1@jhpbooks.net
www.johnhuntpublishing.com
www.6th-books.com

For distributor details and how to order please visit the 'Ordering' section on our website.

Text copyright: Stephanie Sorrell 2011

ISBN: 978 1 84694 611 0

A CIP catalogue record for this book is available from the British Library.

Design: Stuart Davies

Printed and bound by CPI Group (UK) Ltd, Croydon, CR0 4YY
Printed in the USA by Offset Paperback Mfrs, Inc

We operate a distinctive and ethical publishing philosophy in all
areas of our business, from our global network of authors to
production and worldwide distribution.

CONTENTS

Acknowledgements

I am indebted to all those who have, over the years, freely shared their experiences of astral projection with me. And all those pioneers in our Western Culture who have been the trailblazers and pioneers in a wealth of research that has become a solid ground to build on. Amongst these are Muldoon and Carrington, Robert Monroe, Carl Jung, Celia Green, Dr Douglas Baker and Kevin Malarkey.

And thank you, Hanne Jahr, for digging this manuscript out of the shed and persuading me that it deserved to be read. Thank you for your proof reading, Janice. Last but not least, thank you for those spirit teachers and guides who, over the years, gave me guidance, wisdom and protection.

Author's Previous Books

The River that Knows the Way: An Anthology of Wisdom
and Beauty, Science of Thought Press Ltd, 1997
Trusting the Process, Science of Thought Press Ltd, 2000
Depression as a Spiritual Journey, O-Books, 2009
Nature as Mirror, an ecology of body, mind and soul,
O-Books, 2011
Psychosynthesis Made Easy, O-Books, 2011
The Therapist's Cat, Soul Rocks, 2012

Introduction

My interest in astral projection, commonly known as out-of-body experiences (OBEs), began when I was very young. At the age of nine, I had my first experience. My mother and I had moved from Taunton, Somerset to live with my Grandfather in Clacton-on-sea, Essex. I mention this, because as we explore the nature of out-of-body experiences, we will discover that they can happen spontaneously through stress related events that involve major changes in circumstances, as well as reaching puberty, illness and extreme bodily stress as in Near- Death Experiences (NDEs).

I had been at my new Primary school for several weeks and was half skipping, half running with several friends from school. I experienced a sense of excitement and inner happiness which sprang from a sense of belonging in my relatively new environment. The sun was shining and I noticed we were all wearing our check purple and white summer dresses. My friends were chatting excitedly and looking forward to the summer holidays, as was I. Joining in, I shared my sense of expectation for what lay ahead and the sense of freedom long summer holidays endowed us with.

'Suddenly, I was aware of being wrenched away from my friends...

There was a wind in my ears as if I was traveling fast. In no time, I found myself back in my bed at home with my mother standing over me, shaking me hard. "Stephanie— get up!" she urged. "You'll be late for school!"

I blinked at her in disbelief as I fought the urge to be back with my friends, running along the footpath to school. "But…..I *was* up," I argued. "I was talking to Sarah and Jenny. We were…"

"You must have been dreaming," my mother argued. "Come on, you're already late. Hurry up!"

That first event became embedded in my mind for a long time afterwards. All children have a strong sense of right and wrong. As far as I was concerned, I hadn't been asleep dreaming. I had been very much awake and buzzing with the possibilities of what life held for me.'

The second event took place some months later when my Uncle David, whom I had felt especially close to, committed suicide. In the 1960s, the circumstances around his death had been kept a secret as there was still a lot of social shame in this. Lacking a father figure, I had grown to love my uncle who had appeared in my life only recently, having spent most of his time working in South Africa. He was larger than life with a zany sense of humor that made him popular with everyone, especially children.

Memories flooded back from our last time together, one in particular, when he had sat me on his lap, begging my mother to have a little more time with me before he went back to Maidenhead the next day. I remember he had asked me a strange question. "You don't just love me for my money, do you?" he had said.

"No – I love you for you!" I responded urgently.

That was the last physical interchange we had.

Soon after the funeral, when I was in bed, I became aware of a presence that I could only describe as my uncle in the room. Moments later, the bottom of the bed began shaking up and down, just as it would if an adult form was bouncing on the end of it. I knew instinctively that it was my uncle returning to visit me.

Fortunately, my mother not only accepted these experiences, but was fascinated by them. Although a lineage of orthodox ministers existed on one side of the family, there was an equally unorthodox set of relatives on the other side to balance it. Ones that were interested in reincarnation and psychic phenomena!

The next memorable event took place when I was sixteen and on a working holiday with Lydia, a friend from boarding school. The venue of the working holiday was unique. It was Stansted Hall, also known as the Arthur Findlay College in Essex, the home of spiritualism and psychic studies and a venue for those who want to learn more about the subject. We were in the midst of our summer holidays and, we were both waitressing in the dining room for the hordes of visitors who came to the Hall for specialized seminars in clairvoyance and psychic affairs.

Lydia and I were relaxing in our shared room after finishing the supper period of waitressing and I was on my bed resting, allowing my mind to drift....

'Suddenly, I was aware of a vibration in my body, as if I had been plugged into an electrical socket. I tried to speak, or call for help but nothing came out of my mouth as paralysis gripped my body. I heard the sound of my friend opening a can of coke and made my way towards her, overcome with sudden thirst and wanting to have a drink. But my hands passed right through the aluminum of the can and I stared in astonishment as she raised it to her lips again. With effort, because my throat felt strangely constricted, I called her name, but she seemed to ignore me. When I went to touch her, my fingers went straight through her arm as though she wasn't there. I turned back to look at my bed and realized that the figure lying prone on the bed was myself. Inexorably, I found myself back in my body. When asking my friend Lydia if she had noticed anything unusual about me, she said she had only been conscious of me whimpering in my sleep. I think this was when I was trying to speak to her, although my vocal chords had been very tight.'

I experienced other similar cases in my teens. Often, after working a night shift, I would oversleep during the day and astral project onto the ward, notice the new patients and the staff present who seemed totally oblivious of me before someone hammered on my door to tell me that I'd overslept. Appearing on the ward, the new patients whom I had noticed in my astral state would be as I remembered. There were one or two occasions when patients would be sure that I had been on the ward before I had arrived.

I have always been a little absent minded, but the one factor this experience has taught me is to remember the importance of my physical body. And to always question after an extremely vibrant and vivid dream whether I am fully moored in my physical body again. Without it, it would not be possible to do all the things I do, or even be able to communicate this to you in a form you can understand.

During my 20s and 30s, I began to keep a note of my OBEs and, because of this they became clearer and more memorable. Later, I came across the work of psychiatrist, Carl Jung and his exploration into dream work, lucid dreaming and near-death experiences (NDEs). Jung postulated that the act of keeping notes of these experiences imprinted them more firmly within the memory.

During those years of experiential work in the astral world, I journeyed onto the various levels of the astral planes (chapter 2) and met both radiant beings and ones of a darker nature; conversed on an adult level with babies and young children, became caught in a Russian 'astral body trap' and journeyed to a subterranean library in South

America where records were kept of every human soul that had ever been in existence. I have been awed by an outer space experience, humbled by the wisdom stored in the souls of young children, terrified by the dark forces that exist on the lower astral planes with shadows as deep and long as the bright rays existing on the more enlightened planes that communicate through love and wisdom.

I am indebted to pioneers whom I have referred to throughout this work. Pioneers, who have been brave enough to record and validate their work on a scientific, spiritual, psychic level and made it possible for those of us interested in the subject to build on a ground that is substantial rather than nebulous.

My purpose for writing this now, emerges from a need to encourage people to be less afraid of death. Out of all the fears facing us at this time of environmental change and technological revolution, death is still our number one fear. Indeed, my training in psychosynthesis psychology revealed that the three biggest fears of mankind are *death*, *annihilation* and *non-being*. It is possible to see how much of our energy is concerned with building a fortress of beliefs to defend us against the dying process which we perceive as an end state in itself. I have to say that nothing is as easy as making the transition from life to 'so called' death, although the dying process itself can be very uncomfortable. As life on our planet is an ongoing evolutionary process, so the soul that is housed in the physical body continues beyond the physical form. Perhaps that is what we fear the most, not the non-being or that physical death is the end, but the awareness that life goes on as the soul progresses. If we did accept this, we would have to take responsibility for our actions. As Buddhism asserts, every act creates karma, and like the ripples on the lake carry on and on through all eternity.

By nature, we are essentially nomadic. We may not be as tribally nomadic as our ancestors, but few of us can resist the familiar restlessness at the turn of the season as new winds of change sweep in bringing with them fresh impulses. All life forms respond to these powerful transitional forces from the trout returning to their spawning ground, to the vast migratory pathways of the reindeer and caribou, to the homing instincts of the terns and swallows which will navigate perilous distances to reach their destination.

Today, where air travel is still reasonably cheap, but puts a pressure on our environment, we are constantly looking for new methods of harnessing 'clean' energy for navigating these great distances. Yet, on a deeper level, I feel that our obsession with traveling the length and breadth of the earth in our pursuit of novelty is a displaced longing for our spiritual homeland. We are longing for home, for connection with our inner heritage. The beauty of astral projection is that it is free, is environmentally sound and opens up huge landscapes of altered states of consciousness. But as every foreign country has its own unique inscapes, it also has its challenges and dangers which we need to be aware of. If we know that we are traveling to an area that is susceptible to typhoid or TB, we make sure our jabs are up to date. We also get our passport updated, make sure we have the right currency to tender and, either buy the services of a guide, or research the area to highlight dangers that, we as tourists, may be susceptible to. In order to aid us in this we have a map, a guidebook and a compass.

Similarly, the astral world is made up of various planes or levels, largely determined by consciousness, which can be overwhelming if we don't familiarize ourselves with its territory. It also has its hidden dangers. Here, I intend to prepare you for the journeys you may make, and this book is intended as a map for you to follow. If you astral travel and go into areas you have never traveled before, you will want to know the way back if you get lost or encounter difficulty. You will also need to have the right equipment to travel with in the form of familiarity with the terrain and some sort of harness that will still the over-stimulated Western mind. For these reasons, I would ask you *not* to jump to the section of the book on how to astral travel without reading the stages and information in between. By all means, glance at it from time to time, but without a proper understanding of the territory of the astral world, you can meet with experiences that you are not ready to engage with. Although, I can understand the longing to reach the end goal before exploring the beginning, caution is needed too. As one who has astral travelled for many years, I know a little of the territory and the symptoms of something going wrong before it becomes too big to tackle.

Chapter 1

The Astral Body

The idea that human beings possess a double or astral counterpart of the physical body is nothing new. In most ancient cultures, particularly the Egyptian, Tibetan and Mexican ones, there are numerous references to the existence of a 'second' body which can navigate vast distances. In Egypt this was known as the 'Ka', which was a birdlike projection that became detached from the physical body at death. The reason why it was depicted as a bird was due to its ability to fly, soar and float through the air. In *The Tibetan Book of the Dead* there are instructions concerning the release of the astral body after death. They referred to this as a 'radiant' body which was the exact replica of the physical body. Biblically, St Paul refers to a second body when he says; 'There is a natural body and there is a spiritual one.'

A wide spectrum of names has been applied to the astral body, based largely on personal observation, such as 'ethereal' body, because it was believed to be composed of ether. Later, other terms were used to describe this body, such as 'luminous', 'radiant', 'magnetic', 'transparent' and 'fluidic' body became popularly used. Aside from the observations of the projector, many people with psychic ability have witnessed a glowing mist or nebulous shape leaving the body at death. Such a description was given by Joy Snell, a former nurse who looked after the terminally ill, in her book *Ministry of Angels*.

To the average person the astral body is invisible, which is just as well or else life would be even more confusing with astral counterparts popping up all over the place! But for the few who have perceived the astral form, it varies with people's subjective observations. Some perceive it as a luminous sphere or ball, rather than an actual body. American author, Robert Monroe, an experienced astral traveler, described one of his colleagues perceiving it as 'a filmy piece of grey chiffon.' Others have described it as a 'glowing mist' or 'nebulous' shape. Like any human observation there is a wide area for conjecture, just as everyday events seen through the eyes of a cross section of humanity may differ according to perception, mood and experience. But, in the majority of cases, the astral body is perceived as a duplicate of the physical body in shape and outline.

The astral form is very pliable to immediate thoughts and emotions. Its shape, color and movement are largely defined by our emotional state which affects our thoughts. There is one consistent belief among all subjects of OBEs and this is; it is the *consciousness* that leaves the body. The astral body is, in short, a vehicle of consciousness. This consciousness, once detached from the physical body, experiences freedom of movement, has the ability to pass through solid substances like walls and ceilings and can travel at the speed of thought. Additionally, the astral body possesses a sensory system, although the sense organs are not localized in specific areas as in the physical body, but are ubiquitous. For the inexperienced projector the visual aspect may be disturbing at first. In my case, I had to learn to see all over again. This was because many of my first experiences were visually incomprehensible as I would find several images superimposed upon each other. I suppose this is not dissimilar from learning to use a pair of varifocals where an adjustment in the way we see things is needed, or driving a car, or using a hang glider, where a greater degree of skill is called for.

The fact that the astral body can soar up through ceilings suggests that it is weightless. Some people have reported experiencing a 'pull' as if they are held down by a weight. This sensation of being held could be due to the existence of the 'ring-pass-not' which is a psychic barrier that prevents novices from proceeding beyond a particular point, rather like the dividing line in a swimming pool between 'shallow' and 'deep.' As the mind grasps information and knowledge incrementally, so does the technique of astral projection progress and develop with experience. Excitement and fear will compromise the ability to have OBE's, so training oneself to develop a degree of emotional detachment can be very helpful.

Learning from the experiential work of others, as well as my own, the astral body moves in response to the will and desire of the subject. Muldoon and Carrington, two men who studied and mastered the art of astral projection in the 1920s, suggest that it is the unconscious will which is responsible for a projection rather than the conscious will. Although as consciousness increases, the projector can develop a degree of autonomy over where he goes. This I explore more fully in chapter 7.

The silver cord
Although there is a wealth of esoteric literature where there are frequent references to the silver cord, I have never seen mine, despite looking for it, but I am not unique in this. Those who have glimpsed this cord have described it as elasticized with the ability to stretch to any length. Furthermore, there are beliefs of it being attached either to the medulla oblongata at the back of the head, the navel, between the eyes or the solar plexus. Robert Monroe described his silver cord protruding from the shoulder blades. It is quite feasible to think that the silver cord is

joined to any of the major chakras in the body which, in turn, overlay the endocrine glands. The silver cord is often described as the lifeline between the astral and physical body. There is a common belief that if this cord is severed, which is rare, through psychic attack or a physical trauma to the body, death takes place. Since most of us are in life-threatening situations at some point during our life, this is not as bad as it sounds. The circumference of the cord varies according to the distance of the projection, ranging from the width of a little finger to a fine silken thread.

There appears to be no limit to the distance the astral projector can travel on the earth plane. For some individuals it can take many years of sustained effort to travel beyond their own country, or move up to the higher levels of the astral world, as we shall see later. In rare cases, people on a first OBE have traveled out into space or other planets, like Peter Ritchie in chapter 4.

In specialized instances, chiefly recorded by Monroe, the astral body has been able to make an impression on solid substances. But this, understandably, takes a great effort of will and concentration.

On one occasion, Monroe wanted to make a friend of his aware of his presence so that she would remember the contact. He pinched her hard while in his astral form. A few days later, when he saw her again, he followed this up by asking whether she had a bruise on her arm where he had pinched her. She confirmed that she had, much to her surprise, and went on to explain when she had been pinched, which corresponded to the time of his experiment. She remembered because it had given her quite a shock. Although Monroe had spoken to her at the time of pinching her and she had responded, she had no memory of this. Very few people do retain memories of astral communication and I can only assume, as others have before me, that dialogue takes place on another level of consciousness. This makes sense since, although we spend a substantial time dreaming where the contents can seem very real and vivid at the time, yet soon after waking, unless we take the trouble to write them down, they slip far away from conscious memory like pieces of cotton wool. The act of keeping notes, writing down dreams, brings these inner experiences into the foreground. Certainly it was by taking notes and records that psychiatrist Carl Jung was able to recall so much rich content of his dream life. It was for the same reason that Robert Monroe, Sylvan and Muldoon recorded their OBEs. Keeping a diary, and recording dreams and OBEs adds validity to the experiences. Basically, you harvest the work you are willing to put in. Before I move on to the astral world I want to include an incident my grandmother had when her husband, my grandfather, had a life-threatening accident on his way back home.

My grandmother heard my grandfather wheeling his bike up the driveway to put in the shed, just as he always did after a swim. But it was at this exact time that he had been knocked off his bike and rushed to hospital in an ambulance. When the hospital rang to inform her of this, she went out into the shed looking for the bike, thinking they must have mistaken him for someone else. There was no sign of a bike anywhere. Furthermore, after my grandfather had recovered consciousness, he could remember putting his bike away in the shed soon after the swim. On the astral level, perhaps he did!

In sudden accidents the subject is often unaware of what has happened. As concussion and trauma jolt the consciousness out of the physical body, the subject may continue whatever they were doing in the astral state before the accident, oblivious of any separation of the physical body having taken place.

It might be interesting to see how many of the actual 'ghosts' seen by psychic people are actually astral bodies of people who are still very much alive, rather than deceased! Certainly, Monroe was able to perceive the presence of astral bodies floating about in the astral world.

In the next chapter I look at the nature of the astral world and how it is different from the terrestrial one we live in. To do this, I explore the methods of communication which take place between each human subject and its inhabitants.

Chapter 2

The Astral World and its Inhabitants

So, what is the astral world? And how does it differ from our physical world? All geographical places have a map which serves as a guide to the territory.

Whether these maps are primitive or detailed, they do not constitute the terrain itself. Every traveler's experience is unique.

However, my own experiences together with the research I have carried out over the years, seem to reach a conclusion; that there are *different levels* of the astral world. What define these levels are the states of consciousness.

It must be remembered that the astral world is made up of thoughts and emotions. Here, thoughts can attract astral forms, depending on the state of mind. This is a lot more subtle than thought expression in our world, where there may be much thought before a concrete decision is made. Although thoughts make up our self-image in the physical world, this happens over time. If we are disciplined and have a degree of self-awareness we realize that by our thinking we can literally change our lives. Most of the time however, unless we are very self-disciplined and self-aware, thoughts come and go and we feel we have little control over them, especially the more negative and obsessive ones. Similarly, financial circumstances may affect where we live, but what we make out of our terrestrial conditions is largely defined by our thought processes.

Although I had heard the expression, 'thoughts are things' many times throughout my formative years, I didn't realize the full nature and implication of this until I started to astral travel on a regular basis. We know that our thoughts create images in our mind which tap into our emotions. For example, if we are thinking about taking a holiday, we 'imagine' an exotic place with plenty of sunshine and street cafés which bring us a sense of freedom and longing. We want to follow our thoughts and become captured by the image. It was Charles Baudouin, a Swiss psychoanalyst with an interest in autosuggestion, who claimed, 'Every image has in itself a motor-drive.' The holiday image for example, exerts a pull on our emotions, activating a drive to go there. It is interesting that Sigmund Freud's nephew, Ernest Bays, took his uncle's work further by applying his psychological model to the advertising industry. He did this by using images to tap into the sense of lack and failure in people. For example, 'if you buy this wonderful car or face cream, you will feel better and more important.' It continues to work because imagery communicates with us on an unconscious level. It is worthwhile cultivating this seed thought: *Consciousness is defined by our thoughts and the images we pay homage to.*

What are the people like

This is one of the first things we want to know before we visit another country or even somewhere more localized such as another village, town or city.

Although areas of the world can be defined by productivity, urban or rural, prosperity or impoverishment, it does not apply to the astral world. This is because the astral world corresponds to levels of consciousness. It is a little like one's circle of friends being made up of work and sports colleagues to ones with a similarity of values and interests. However, if we go through a lot of internal changes like the loss of a loved one, a life-threatening illness or even a transpersonal experience, our consciousness changes so that we attract different people to us. In turn, unless our old friends are able to change with us, they drop away. This is because our energy is magnetizing different people and circumstances into our orbit and deflecting others.

When I worked as Editor for a spiritual magazine, formerly *Science of Thought Review* (later *New Vision*), the founder, Hamblin's motto was: 'Change your thinking, change your life.' This had certainly happened for him as Hamblin had spent the first half of his life working as an optician in Wigmore Street, London, correcting people's *outer* vision. Ironically, the second part of his life was concerned with changing people's *inner* vision. He moved from a place of worldly vision to an inner place of spiritual vision. But, for this change to occur there is often a major catalyst that precipitates change. In Hamblin's case, the catalyst was the death of his son at the age of ten.

This was also true for a young soldier, George Ritchie, who is mentioned in chapter 4 on near-death experiences. Before the illness that actually caused him to die for nine minutes, although interested in becoming a doctor as a result of witnessing his father's painful death from rheumatoid arthritis, he became preoccupied with the wealth that such a career would bring. His consciousness was hooked into the desire level, where he longed for a Cadillac and a glamorous life. But after his near-death experience (NDE), as the narrative of his story unfolds, he discovers that people who have died found themselves in a world largely corresponding to the state of consciousness they lived in before they died. He understood that it was just as much about the quality of heart underlying the actions as the actions themselves. For example, if someone was engaged in good works, but their hearts were centered on arrogance, thinking that they were better than the people they helped, this would counteract the intention. What lay in a person's heart was more important than what a person was 'seen' to be doing. For example, a jobless person on benefit who occupies their day picking up rubbish or performing acts of kindness without the intention for self-promotion or being acknowledged, can be at a much higher level of consciousness than someone running a large charity who may feel smug about themselves and their work. Desire for position and money might fuel the drive that gets us to the top of our profession, but not so in the astral world where these same drives may hook us into the lower levels that are peopled by ambition and greed.

Dwelling on these lower levels of the astral world are also souls locked into a seedy underworld of drugs such as alcohol and other mind altering and addictive substances. Opinions may be what define our personality in this life and earn us a certain amount of position and respect, but in the astral world they imprison us and become milestones in our ability to move forward and upward. As in the physical world, we can become imprisoned by the very things we think will set us free. Greed and resentment is the imprisoning force, holding things lightly is the key here.

We all know how thoughts can inspire, elevate and lift us out of our seemingly mundane lives. Yet, they can also have the opposite effect of imprisoning us and making us slave to their influence as do obsessively negative thoughts. If we feel powerless to control them, then they really rule us, making our lives a misery. One of the opportunities we are faced with in this life is being able to control our thoughts, rather than allowing them to control us. Thoughts are, in actuality, servants of the mind.

Basically there are three main levels to the astral world.

These are:

Lower astral
Planes of desire
The Summerland

Lower astral

We know that the physical world is made up of layers of matter, ranging from dense minerals which constitute the earth's crust and from which minerals such as lead, iron and titanium can be extracted. Held within these substances are liquids and gases. It is the same in the astral world where each 'stratum' of matter possesses its own unique characteristics and 'climate' through which the astral traveler gains entry. The more dense strata of the astral world are believed to extend far into the earth's crust. Maybe this is where the Greek legend of the under-world, the home of Pluto or Hades, originated. Persephone, the Greek Goddess, who spent several months of the year in the underworld, was believed to reside here with the God, Pluto. The underworld has also been connected with deep depression where mythological figures like Persephone, spent time in the underworld each year before emerging, wiser, to bring back spring and blossom to the earth. Sadly, what is often forgotten is the fact that Pluto was the God of treasure and wealth. I believe this to be a metaphor for wisdom and inner wealth. Very often, people who have undergone an underworld initiation, possess an inner wisdom as if the pain they have endured has given birth to depth and meaning. This is soul treasure, pure alchemy. Depression is really a rite of passage into the underworld as defined in my book, *Depression as a Spiritual Journey.*

Because the lower astral levels are devoid of light, they

can be peopled by helpless, self-punishing and lost souls. When first I began to consciously astral project at the age of sixteen, on several occasions I found myself in the lower astral realms. It was an unnerving experience. I felt as though I was being sucked down and down into a marshy swamp. In the darkness, although I was hovering some distance above them, I saw ugly deformed creatures who were chanting a hypnotic incomprehensible language. I instinctively edged away as they reached towards me with ugly grimy hands. I was terrified they would grab me and drag me down with them. The experience seemed more intensely real than a nightmare.

Yet – each time I visited this realm, I was aware of the presence of someone I can only describe as a guide or teacher. They were not of this lower astral realm, because there was a light and peace about them that did not seem to have a place here. I assume that the 'guide' took me to this realm for a purpose. Afterwards, I had an overwhelming sense that, despite my initial repulsion and fear, I should extend love to these creatures as it was the only force which could lift them out of their misery. These early experiences in astral projection had a lasting and sobering effect upon me. Often, I would fight against astral projection for fear of undergoing similar experiences again and, even worse, become stranded on these dark planes. Fortunately, this has not been the case. I have since learned that this lower level is made up of beings who, through their behavior on the earth and the lives they led, have through their thoughts, desires and inner darkness confined themselves here. It is only an awakening in consciousness that will set them free. That is why love and compassion is so important in their evolution and healing process.

The planes of desire

Desire plays a strong part in where the astral projector ends up. Desire is like the rudder on a ship. It sets the course and directional pull of where we are bound. Basically, there is nothing wrong with desire, unless we become slave to it. Desire can be a longing or calling to undertake some work or course of study in life. It can be the desire to undertake a grueling trek across the globe or to be instrumental in setting up a charity, to have children, foster animals or recover from some long term illness or accident. Within that desire is the will which, if aligned to the mental or spiritual values, create the energy to undertake some worthwhile work or service. Bringing anything into form is never easy because we live in a world of duality where the forces of light and darkness test our vision and strength. When the will is compromised by greed for ownership and power, the energy becomes darker and coarser. As the forces of light recede and the darker aspect of the will comes into force, the lower astral level becomes activated. Desire becomes tarnished by darker forces for which the owner ultimately pays a heavy price. The gold of the seed kernel is replaced by coarser, heavier material. This is because each desire activates a course of intention where we have already made choices about the outcome and how it will affect others. This next level of the astral world is the one which penetrates our everyday life. Our surroundings, whether we are in our own house or someone else's, will look the same as they do when we are in our physical body. The only difference is that solid matter is no longer an obstacle. We can just move through structures as if they were made of air. We will be able to see relatives, friends and passersby as they go about their business. Many of whom we know in everyday life will not respond to us. It is as if we are invisible, which we are to many. Children are likely to see astral projectors as they are less conditioned by the world to see only what they want to see.

I include several personal experiences which I had in my 20s, illustrating this interaction with young children.

January 1979:8-8.30am

'I was lying on my tummy when I lifted out of my body.

...Passed up through the ceiling and through the roof of the house. Then, in a horizontal position, I floated past some blocks of houses. Next, I found myself in a large hall filled with people and was drawn to a baby in a pram, as it seemed to be the only one in the room who could see or acknowledge my presence. In moments, I saw the baby's astral counterpart leave its physical body then float over towards me.

I held the baby in my arms and some form of communication took place between us. Neither of us spoke as it was more a telepathic understanding. I remember thinking how strange it was at the time, to find myself communicating freely with a baby who claimed to be eighteen months old, yet in the physical body could only make burbling noises. He communicated that his mother had died, and that his father who was sitting close to the pram in conversation with another man, had very little love for his son. The baby expressed his unhappiness at this, and appeared to be very sensitive towards his father's problems. He went on to explain that he had come into incarnation to pioneer some service in order to help humanity, although he didn't divulge any more about the nature of his work to me. Before leaving, I promised I would try to visit him again.

There were a few other events taking place in the hall which attracted my attention, such as a skirmish between two youths, but they didn't hold my interest so I left them.

Next, I found myself gliding along a street in an area which was unfamiliar to me. At one point, I communicated with a middle-aged woman. I was a little surprised that she could see me, but thought perhaps she was psychic or astral traveling herself. The whole experience had taken little longer than half an hour.'

About three weeks later, I had another astral projection which was connected to this experience.

January 25th 1979. 7.30 am
'Experienced five consecutive lift-outs.

One involved passing through the roof of the house, as usual, but looking up at the night sky to witness three or four lights darting across the dark heavens which then vanished into a vast mother ship, shaped like a wheel.

The most vivid recollection was of a woman with a northern accent. Initially, I heard her voice when I was in the cataleptic state, then I found myself sitting at a table with other young people opposite this woman who referred to us all as her 'students'. She looked to be in her mid thirties with fair shortish hair, a fringe and thick eyebrows. I appeared to be asking her questions.

"When can I see the boy again?" I asked, referring to the baby I had been communicating with recently.

"Not just yet." The woman looked directly at me. "You must understand that it is difficult for your vibration to be in harmony with visiting these special old souls. Your mind has to be clear of negative, depressing thoughts. Watching television and being influenced by certain books greatly hinder contact with these special souls. You have a choice... always a choice."

"What's that?"

"You can be with them all the time, or only when your vibrations are right."

"What do you mean? That I die?"

"Yes... But it is your soul who makes the choice, not you – your personality."

This is where the conversation ended. The woman then handed me a tumbler of purple liquid with gold flakes floating in it. She insisted that it was medicinal and that I should drink it as it was 'my color'.

When the woman referred to disturbing films, I remembered I had watched a horror film the night before and was reading a murder mystery. From experience, I know that the thoughts that you fill your mind with have an impact on astral projection. If all life is held within an energetic field, and that by taking drugs and filling our minds with negativity compromises a healthy state of consciousness, this makes sense.

After this projection, I awoke with a splitting headache, which is not uncommon for me if I have astral traveled. I always put it down to changes in consciousness, rather like jet lag after covering a vast distance in a relatively short space of time.

Many people who astral travel have reported seeing their surroundings shimmering and vibrating as though alive. Others have described luminosity. In the astral world there is no such thing as night and day, as apart from the lower astral levels, there is an almost numinous appearance to everything.

The Summerland

The 'Summerland' is an expression that was adopted by Theosophists, Wiccans and Spiritualists to define an idyllic resting place between lifetimes. It is a heavenly place where there is no judgment or obstacles to confront. It is the highest point of the astral world, where there are likely to be transpersonal experiences. The Summerland is a transitional place where there is reunion with loved ones and a celebration of arriving 'home' in the heaven world. On this level, there are likely to be many angelic beings, guides and teachers who will work towards orientating the newly arrived soul to their changed life. As there is no sense of time as we know it in the astral world, it is not possible to say how long anyone will remain there once they have passed away. It could be months or years.

Sometimes an astral traveler will find themselves in the Summerland and perhaps want to linger for a while because it is so peaceful and harmonious, but it is usually only a brief period despite the natural impulse to want to linger in such a harmonious place.

Often, people who have had near-death experiences (NDEs) find themselves here and have reported that they had a choice of remaining there or returning to their physical body. Any NDE is life changing and will impact on the subject's future decisions and choices. Most important of all is the awareness that one does not have to fear death. Life is ongoing and largely defined by the choices that are made and the stream of thoughts which constitute consciousness. Everything we think and do now, impacts on our future.

Interestingly enough, the upper level of the astral world is not just confined to the deceased or those experiencing NDEs. It can be attained through a longing for spiritual connection and those who have worked hard to refine their level of consciousness. But there are often incidents where a materially minded person may access them as a one off. Yet—nothing happens by chance. If a change of consciousness is needed for the subject to change their perception, an astral projection experience will fulfill this need.

According to my recorded accounts there appear to be

fewer thought forms and less negative emotional content at this level. Instead, there is a heightening in consciousness. Usually, those who attain this level, have some degree of spiritual consciousness or purity. As one journeys into this upper level, they become less identified with personal problems belonging to the mundane or material world. In a sense, the mind becomes more refined.

Sandwiched between the upper stratum of the astral world and the mental level are various schools and colleges of learning where souls can study their area of interest. This learning is never imposed on anyone. Rather, the individual experiences a deepening longing to find out more about the world they find themselves in and also the subjects that interested them in earthly life, yet perhaps, never had the opportunity to explore. People who have visited these levels have reported seeing buildings bathed in gold or a shimmering translucence. Often the light is dazzling. I have visited these places myself, especially those areas focused on the arts. These are also the product of thought, where many have contributed to their formation. In fact, there are people throughout history, and even today, who have been actively involved in the expression of the arts that have visited these buildings in their sleep state and drawn inspiration from them, even though memory of them may have been lost within the transition to waking consciousness. Additionally, there are schools of science and architecture where subjects who have visited them in their astral form, return to waking consciousness with an idea or invention, whose time has come, to work its way into matter.

Anyone who has ever glimpsed these higher astral levels, will awaken with a longing to return again. Although the use of drugs may facilitate the awareness of these higher levels, there is no easy way to travel there or retain the memories. Sadly, there are some whose use of drugs or challenging earthly circumstances leave them open to a sense of 'divine homesickness'. They withdraw further and further from the physical world through drugs and end their life in an effort to reach these longed for levels again. But there are no shortcuts. Those who have taken their own life may remain trapped in the lower realms of the astral world until their time has come, although I have to say these souls are never alone. There are always helpers and guardians around to comfort and lend a hand to these lost souls.

So the astral world is made of several groups of inhabitants:

Helpers
Guides
The recently deceased
Astral forms of humans still alive in the physical world
Non-human inhabitants
Debris

To those who ask 'does everyone astral travel?' I cannot answer this, or be more specific. I have learned that the physical body needs to rest and draw in its own life force and it can only do this by separating consciousness from the body. Memory of out-of-body experiences takes place when waking consciousness is maintained throughout this transition. In most cases, when individuals sleep, their astral body separates from the physical form and hovers in the air not far from the physical body. This accounts for the flying, floating, falling dreams which many of us experience alongside the sudden jolt we have as we wake up too suddenly. Many also go to the higher realms of learning or to the Summerland.

Helpers

In every area of life there *are* helpers and guides, although these are not the same. Helpers are those who volunteer to aid those struggling in darkness on the astral planes or who have come for a special purpose. They have not yet "qualified" to the level of guides. Most people have helpers and guides while on the earth. The guide is long term, keeping the link with souls often through several incarnations. Helpers may stay for one particular task, then move away. Their compassion may stem from having experienced a similar struggle with drugs or letting go of resentment and malice while on the earth and have, over time, transcended their desires. Often, when souls have experienced and 'worked through' their selfishness, they develop a need to help those who are trapped in the same position they were once in. These include those who, while embodied on the earth, have created great unhappiness for others in the physical world and are locked into guilt, fear and further malice. There are others who, through drinking and excessive sexuality, find it impossible to move away from the lower levels because of the extent they are hooked in at the desire level. Those who have committed acts of violence and cruelty while embodied in earthly incarnation, spend time on the lower levels until they show remorse for the unhappiness they caused and seek to make amends for their cruel acts.

Guides

Guides are evolved teachers whose compassion and wisdom make them available to those who have the will to move on, to heal and learn more. Then there are the angels who come from the upper levels of the mental world and clothe themselves in an astral body when they reach the astral world. They do this because their radiance would be too much for those on the lower astral planes. They are there to guide those who are preparing to move on to the next level beyond the astral world, the mental one.

Non human inhabitants

The non human inhabitants include thought forms which can build up a very real presence, kept alive and animated by those attracted to them.

Within this non human matrix, I would include animals. Animals, because of their level of consciousness and innocence, move through the astral world quickly. Their life on the earth is relatively brief compared to ours and after a period of orientation they leave the astral planes very quickly and join the 'animal group soul' where they prepare for their continued evolution. Domestic animals that are more individualized may remain in the astral world for a little longer before moving on to their own training schools of progression.

Many people with a longing to help those in need, whether animal or human beings, may become astrally active during the chaos of an earthquake, tsunami or volcanic explosion which have killed and traumatized thousands of people. These individuals can awake with vivid memories of their 'work' within the astral world; sometimes going as far as relating lucid accounts where they have been helping others. These activities will be experienced as dreams even before the news of a world disaster has reached the media.

Debris

The detritus or discarded matter of the astral world is made up of thought forms that are dying and have outlived their usefulness. Then there are the 'astral shells' which souls moving onto the mental plane have left behind

29

and no longer need. Although sometimes an active thought form will seize hold of an astral shell and use it for a while before it becomes too unrecognizable. Gradually, like any discarded matter, they break down and are subject to a recycling process just as they are here.

So we can see that the astral world is not necessarily a wonderful peaceful place to visit. Protection is needed while astral projecting. There are those trained in the magic of the dark arts who seek to cause fear and unpleasantness where they can. A seatbelt of protective light is needed, whether it is God, or some other meaningful force for good. I explore this more fully in chapter 7.

Chapter 3

Symptoms Accompanying Astral Projection

There are several universally accepted symptoms of an astral projection. These, as a rule, actually precede the exteriorization of the astral body. Since one in ten people experience some or most of these symptoms prior to an astral projection, it is worth unpacking and familiarizing ourselves with them here.

Symptoms manifesting before astral projection

Buzzing or roaring in the head
Vibrating in the body
Paralysis of the body/catalepsy
Sound of voices nearby
Loud explosion, popping sounds
Sensation of the eyeballs turning upwards
Rapid heartbeat

The first and most common symptom that occurs is an auditory one, where the subject hears a buzzing, ringing, roaring or humming sound rather like a generator. This initial sound is repetitious, almost hypnotic in nature. As time passes, it may become progressively louder until it causes physical discomfort, as it creates a build-up of pressure in the head. These vibrational waves tend to fluctuate according to the level of relaxation. Other symptoms of this nature are banging, thumping, and explosive sounds.

On a tactile level, the skin may feel irritated or as if it is prickling. Finally, the subject will experience a sense of muscular paralysis when the physical body appears to be rendered powerless. This is known as the cataleptic state, a temporary period of bodily paralysis which is necessary to stop us acting out our dreams and sleep walking.

By this time, the roaring sound will have become unbearable. The heartbeat may increase and the breathing alters. Sometimes there is a sense of being split in two – which is precisely what is taking place as the astral body is attempting to separate from the physical one. This is a little reminiscent of the sensations experienced while a plane is taking off. Just as the roar and speed seems almost unbearable, the plane takes off. It is the same with astral projection.

I include a few of my own experiences here and, later, those of other subjects who were kind enough to fill in my questionnaire.

January 7 1979: Mine
'Had a number of projections, always preceded by the loud roar in my ears, increasing in volume until it seemed to be deafening. My eyes rolled uncontrollably upwards, and then my limbs became paralyzed. Maintained awareness of lifting in and out of my physical body, although events in between were hazy and not worth recording.'

January 17 1979: Mine
'Throughout the course of the night, I had three distinct 'lift outs' accompanied by the usual cataleptic state. In each case, I disliked the violent vibrational shaking and became fearful. Eventually, after what seemed an endless amount of effort, I forced myself back into my physical body by practicing various breathing exercises. It left me feeling tired and drained. An important observation in between

lift-outs was a brilliant flash of light which seemed to illumine the whole room. At the time, I was in the cataleptic state. When I came to and looked for the source of light, thinking it was lightning, I could find none. The light was so brilliant that it was blinding.'

February 1 1980: Mine

'Lift-out proceeded by tickling sensation in all my limbs, becoming increasingly more uncomfortable as I was in the cataleptic state and couldn't scratch! Also a mild vibrating pull. At the moment of lifting out I saw various unfamiliar shapes pass across my astral vision. One of these shapes resembled a clock with spiral patterns etched on the back. Next, I was aware of racing along a dark corridor at great speed so that everything became blurred. I paused outside a door and something prompted me to open it and go inside, although another part of me was against the idea and I also felt anxiety for my physical body, so I awoke. This concern for my body's welfare was due to a blocked nose and I was having difficulty breathing.'

Sylvan Muldoon 1920s

Muldoon, one of the great pioneers investigating the nature of astral projection in the 1920s, had his first experience when he was twelve years old. After being asleep for a few hours, he awoke to find that he was suspended between movement and sleep. He was quite obviously in the cataleptic state. He described that he had an awareness of existing somewhere. A 'somewhere' he had never experienced before. It felt as though his body was 'glued' to the bed, and he was unable to move for some time. He remembered thinking how strange it was to be fully conscious, yet unable to move. Next, after the catalepsy had passed, he felt as though he was floating;

then he was aware of a vibration in his body. At one point, he saw that his physical body was still in bed and thought that he must be going mad. He saw a silver cord which joined his two bodies together. He moved through the rooms of the house, his surprise steadily mounting as he witnessed his body moving as liquid through solid structures.

On returning to his physical body, once again he experienced the cataleptic state accompanied by the vibrating, followed by a sharp pain in his body as though had been split in two.

Ramana Maharshi

Hindu Spiritual leader, Ramana Maharshi, gives an account of how, once, when he was lying down fully conscious, he felt his astral body rising progressively higher into the air. He was able to see the objects below him gradually diminishing in size. He described entering a vast expanse of radiant light. He then moved back into alignment with his physical body.

Symptoms of exteriorization

A sense of speeding through the air
Astral wind
Experience of a dark tunnel with light at the end
Brilliant light
Fingers passing through solid matter
Seeing one's own physical body below
Seeing one's astral body
Feelings of euphoria

Subjects will feel as if they are being pulled upwards by a powerful invisible force. Some people have described this ascension as 'spiraling' or 'zigzagging' in nature. For a few moments, at a distance of several meters, the astral body hovers over the physical body as if preparing itself for the next stage. From this viewpoint, the subject may see their own body below them and looking around seeing their familiar surroundings from an aerial perspective. After some clumsy experimentation, the subject will quickly discover that their new body is weightless, able to pass through matter and capable of traveling at incredible speed to various places known and unknown. Prior to complete exteriorization there is often an experience of racing along a dark, extensive tunnel and then emerging into a bright field of light, although this seems to be more symptomatic of NDEs. Usually, after the initial panic, subjects report experiencing a greater lucidity of mind accompanied by feelings of well-being, peace and euphoria. I include here some individual accounts of spontaneous projection from questionnaire volunteers.

Irene from Devon writes:

'... I awoke one night from sleep and thought that I had alighted from bed. The movement was so natural, because sometimes when I awoke, I would make myself a hot drink then go back to sleep. As I crossed the room towards the door to go into the kitchen, I reached for the light switch and found that I couldn't press it because my hand had passed right through it. I remembered thinking, "I must be still asleep and dreaming this." Looking down at the rest of me, expecting to see the bed covers, I discovered I was positioned upright on the floor, but dressed in what looked to be a white gown (which I didn't possess). I felt a vague sort of panic, thinking I was experiencing a nightmare and walked in the direction of the bed. Instead, I seemed to glide above the floor level. Suddenly, I heard a loud knock at the front door and, in an instant, was somehow transported to standing on the mat behind the door.

Outside the door was a man wearing a cloth cap. Although I hadn't opened the door, I could somehow see through it as though it didn't exist. The man said, "I am Peter, please come with me." As he spoke, I heard my baby daughter crying in her cot and instantly, at the speed of thought, I was back in my bedroom looking anxiously at the cot from the far side of the room. My surroundings were bathed in a soft weird glow. A great panic gripped me and, from the little I had read about people who had 'died' and recovered, informed me that my 'spirit' had left my body. Who would look after my baby? Then I must have gone back to sleep, because the next time I awoke it was daylight.'

Symptoms preceding return to the physical body

Catalepsy/paralysis along with the fear of not being able to return to physical body
Vibrating
Headache
Lethargy/drowsiness
Feelings of vitality and freshness
Euphoria
Quickened heartbeat

These symptoms are fairly similar to the ones manifesting before exteriorization as both are related to making the transition in or out of the physical body. The experience of a headache, although common, is transitory and passes after a few minutes. Feelings of well-being and vitality appear to manifest more in people who have been or are ill.

Fear of not being able to get back to the physical body

Although a number of writers on astral projection have dismissed fears of not being able to get back to the physical body as unfounded, this is a very *real* fear. And here I refer to other people's experience as well as my own. Having been in that transitional cataleptic state which often precedes astral projection as it does just before returning to it, I know how frightening this can be. When this first started happening, I worried about people thinking that I was dead if they found me unresponsive or being buried alive.

Irene from Devon explains:

'A rather unpleasant incident occurred one night when I had fallen asleep with the light on. I had been working very hard that day and had suddenly come over weary. I awoke with a start, only to find that I couldn't move. This applied only to my physical body, as my astral or 'spiritual' body was threshing about like a fish out of water in its attempts to get back to the physical body. Something had gone wrong with the normal procedure of waking up. Not knowing very much about out-of-body mechanics, as I hadn't deliberately practiced it, real fear gripped me as I strained to move my body, but couldn't even blink or move an eyelash.

I searched my mind for all the study I had made on spiritual phenomena and psychic matters and remembered reading something a psychic researcher had written about this. He had said that should one find oneself in the position of being 'locked out' from one's body, to make a great mental effort to lift just a little finger. I carried out these instructions and, thankfully, there was an instant snapping back into place of the two bodies. Shakily, I got up and appeared to feel no worse for the experience. It was, however, a very eerie and frightening incident. I have learned since that this is quite a common occurrence amongst people who have astral traveled.'

Since any transpersonal experience involves consciousness, it makes sense that we all interpret these OBEs according to our level of mental, emotional and spiritual understanding. Some people will want to push it away as a bad dream. It is possible that the acceptance of what has taken place as a reality, would involve an uncomfortable breakdown of our whole belief system. Others will be fascinated by the event and want to find out more about it. But these experiences, once acknowledged, are life changing, attracting different conditions into the individual orbit.

Chapter 4

Near-Death Experiences

According to a recent article in New Scientist, 18 million Americans have had a near-death experience (NDE). Some of these were experienced during a cardiac arrest, although the majority came as a result of fainting. Neurologist, Kevin Nelson, describes in his book, *The Spiritual Doorway*, how the brain enters a state of 'hybrid consciousness' where it slips into a borderland between dreaming and wakefulness.

NDEs are incidents where people who have apparently died, even been announced clinically dead, to only spontaneously recover consciousness several minutes later. Others, who have been critically ill and been on the point of making the transition from life to death, have made a miraculous recovery. Many of these people have spoken afterwards of becoming aware of angelic beings who have taken them on a journey to the 'other side', often described as a realm of light or heaven. Those who have returned to their physical bodies and obviously recovered, have been so inwardly changed by their NDE that their whole life has been transformed and illumined by this 'realer than life' experience. I include some of them in this chapter. One of my main sources of material is based on the work of George Ritchie, who was a soldier during the Second World War. Also I refer to a much more recent case involving American, Kevin Malarkey and his six year old son, Alex, who died for nine minutes. Later, he wrote a book, aptly called, *The boy who came back from heaven* and his meeting with God and his angels. Both cases richly describe the plains of heaven and how this near-death experience was life changing to both the soldier and young boy. Indeed Ron Moody, the psychiatrist, who through his interest in parapsychology, became the pioneer in bringing NDE's into the public domain, was richly inspired by George Ritchie's experiences. Furthermore, he was motivated to write his bestselling book, *Life after Life*, which drew on extensive research in the area of NDEs. After interviewing over a thousand people who had had NDEs, he was convinced of the validity of an existence after death.

Although the symptoms experienced by NDEs are similar to those who astral project, they are unique in that they are both life changing and life affirming. It has been estimated that 4 million Americans have had a NDE, but have chosen to keep a low profile about this because of the fear of ridicule.

Symptoms of a near-death experience

- Vision of deceased loved one's and relatives
- Meeting with angelic beings
- A frequent experience of racing along a tunnel
- Feelings of great peace, joy, love and freedom
- Life review where there may be a choice of whether to return to the physical body to undertake a work that will be beneficial to mankind
- Feelings of detachment at having left the physical body
- Reluctance to return to the physical body
- A renewed sense of meaning and purpose following the experience
- A transpersonal experience such as a meeting with an angelic or wise being that totally changes our viewpoint and direction in life

- Inability to live inside the parameters of our limited viewpoint before the experience

George Ritchie, a British soldier in 1943

Ritchie collapsed in an army hospital where he was placed in an isolation unit with acute double pneumonia. Within 24 hours his breathing had stopped with no perceptible heartbeat, pulse or blood pressure. He was pronounced dead. But while his body was being prepared for the morgue, the orderly thought he saw a hand move. The doctor, on being informed, once again pronounced him as dead. The orderly, still puzzled, suggested that Ritchie should be given an adrenalin injection. This was carried out. Immediately afterwards, Ritchie's heart began to beat again. This was nine minutes after he had been declared dead for the second time.

While Ritchie's body was being prepared for the morgue, the young soldier found himself looking down at himself. The first thing he saw was the body partially covered in a white sheet. He noticed the grey pallor of his face and slack jaw. Realizing that it was his own body, he frantically tried to draw back the sheet from the body but failed. He then became aware of a brilliant light filling the room. Within this light he saw what he described as 'Christ.' Then he saw his life appear before him in a series of pictures. Next, Christ had asked him what he had done with his life while on the earth. Shortly afterwards, he seemed to enter another dimension where he was surrounded by crowds of people drinking and smoking on the earth and spirits hovering nearby desperately trying to get hold of a cigarette or alcoholic drink to feed the addiction they had died of while on earth. He was also shown groups of people locked in verbal combat over religion and politics and even trying to kill each other for their beliefs.

The foreground changed to one where there were state-of-the-art universities and laboratories which reminded him of something from a science fiction novel. He saw a city composed of light. Here were people who were studying hard. When Ritchie asked Christ if this was heaven, he was told that they were people who had moved beyond their own selfish needs and wanted to further the good in the world. Then he was taken to another dimension far out in space where there was a shining city where love predominated. He assumed this was heaven, but was not allowed to enter.

When Christ began to show him the future of the world, Ritchie became drowsy and he saw his body and knew that he had to get back into it for he had a work to do.

This experience was life-changing for the soldier. He gave up his preoccupation with prestige and wealth and concentrated on becoming a doctor and psychiatrist in his determination to help people.

Tony
A security guard who collapsed at a hospital with an acute heart attack described how, after everything had blacked out, he found himself floating somewhere above his body. From his vantage point, he watched his physical body being lifted onto a stretcher then, later, he saw a doctor bring his fist hard down on his chest to shock his heart into action. He noticed various trolleys of equipment and machines around him and overheard people talking. When electrical shocks were applied to his body, he said his body jumped up into the air then, moments later, he was back in his body. He also said he felt that he had a free choice whether to return to his body or not.

Lydia

A woman of 39, after suffering a pulmonary embolism following an emergency operation, reports how she became aware of her consciousness rising up into the air above her bed. She experienced a sense of exhilaration.

But later, with detached puzzlement, she watched the doctor thumping her chest and someone else injecting something into her heart. Then a nurse rushed to the bed and accidently knocked over the drip stand so that the end of it caught the side of her face. Witnessing this, Lydia experienced no alarm, as in her astral body she couldn't feel any pain. She was jerked back into alignment with her physical body by the voice of the doctor shouting and ordering her to breathe.

Later, her observations were confirmed when she discovered that she had been given an injection into her heart. She also had a bruise over her left eye in precisely the same spot where she had witnessed the drip stand striking her.

Mrs Torbuck of Devon

This lady had been discharged from hospital following an operation when, a few days later, she had hemorrhaged badly and been rushed back to hospital. Her condition was so grave that she was pronounced clinically dead, a fact her sister passed onto her some days later when she came to visit.

But Mrs Torbuck's experience of that time had been very different:

'She had been conscious of standing outside looking through the window of the ward, watching the team of medical personnel working on her. Although it was night time when this happened, she was aware of being in sunny surroundings. She also became aware that she could see all around her without moving her head. Gradually, the light around her became more brilliant and seemed to emanate a feeling of great love. She described this feeling as being so powerful that it was impossible to describe.

The next thing she was aware of was waking the next day in the hospital bed, after having had a blood transfusion. The Ward Sister then informed her that she had died, but had been fortunate enough to recover through the efforts of the hospital team.

Although she had never been religious before, after the experience she felt sure there was a God. She was also aware of a growing tingling in her hands and even felt them burning. Soon afterwards, Mrs Torbuck enrolled on a healing course after discovering that she had this gift.'

Iris Zelam

Iris, a Grammar school teacher, was recovering from major heart surgery in the intensive care unit when she suddenly experienced a sharp pain in her chest. She heard one of the doctors' remark, 'We've lost her!'

Next, she was aware of a white mist surrounding her physical body. She became this mist and watched the doctors operating on her chest. Her consciousness then entered a dark tunnel, at the end of which was brilliant light. She had an overwhelming longing to unite with the light and found herself surrounded by unfamiliar spirit people. Finally, it was her sense of responsibility towards her husband that caused her to return reluctantly to her physical form. Also, an unfamiliar authoritarian voice informed her immediately afterwards that she had made the right decision.

George of London

A business man whose heart stopped, remembered rising

up out of his body and seeing his physical body lying motionless below him, surrounded by doctors and nurses. One of them was applying compressions to his chest; another tied a tourniquet around his leg. He remembered a period of darkness, rather like passing through a dark tunnel, then emerging into the light. As the light became more brilliant, he saw clouds and blue sky. A voice seemed to tell him that he had to return to his body. Reluctantly, and with great disappointment, he did so.

'The boy who went to heaven and came back.'
Alex Marlarkey, six year old son of Kevin Malarkey, USA, 2004.

This is a unique modern day case of a NDE involving a six year old boy who not only remembers the experience, but has an ongoing dialogue with 'angels' and the heaven world. His father, fully supported him in his experience and was inspired to write a book, *The boy who went to Heaven and came back.* This includes excerpts of his son Alex's experiences.

The NDE happened as the result of a major car accident where the vehicle was hit violently by another car. As a result, Alex's father was thrown through the glass window while Alex was trapped in the car with a severed spine from the neck downwards. The boy describes the incident with great clarity.

'For just one second before all the 'action' began, there was a moment of calmness. I remember thinking someone was going to die. When the calm ended, I heard the sound of glass breaking, and I saw Daddy's feet going out of the car.

Now I thought I knew who was going to die. But then I saw something unbelievably cool. Five angels were carrying Daddy outside the car. Four were carrying his body, and one was supporting his neck and head. The angels were big and muscular, like wrestlers, and they had wings on their backs from their waists to their shoulders. I thought Daddy was dead, but it was okay because the angels were going to make him okay.... The fireman cut my seatbelt off because it was jammed. They put something in my throat to make me breathe...... I went through a long, white tunnel that was very bright. I didn't like the music in the tunnel; it was really bad music played on instruments with really long strings.... But then I got to heaven, and there was powerful music, and I loved it.'

Alex's dialogue with Jesus and the angels was ongoing as, he claimed, he spent a lot of his time visiting the heaven world which he describes, succinctly through his writings in much the same way as George Ritchie. With greater internet access, it is possible to keep and update of Alex Malarkey's progress through u-tube.

Chapter 5

Journeys in Outer Space and Other Dimensions

Admittedly, there is a bit of an overlap here with journeying into space and a NDE because, most of the time, these transpersonal experiences are enmeshed. NDEs and otherworldly experiences are surreal and hard to capture in words.

These next four experiences of astral projection took place in the 1980s. Although I did not record the first one, it remains clear in my memory because it was so vivid. It is also what can be called a transpersonal experience, as it bypasses our everyday known and named experience, evoking feelings of peace, love, beauty and awe.

'Initially, I was aware of being in some sort of spacecraft and hurtling through space. I was aware of a trustworthy presence with me who appeared to be in control of the spacecraft. We passed through swathes of dark space and pathways of shining stars. At one point I was aware of 'standing' before a vast panorama of stars, glittering in a myriad of colors. The sense of vastness and majesty was breathtakingly beautiful. Then there was a voice beside me that said, "That is the One-Eyed Wolf Galaxy", and as I stared, I could see the shape of the wolf and his one glittering eye. At the time, I remember thinking that I must look out for this galaxy in the media.'

Much later, during this time of the Hubble Space Telescope, I am still waiting for this discovery to be made!

This second OBE took place in 1980 which involved traveling to a Russian laboratory.

'I was aware of an uncomfortable tickling sensation before lift-out. Then I was aware of a holy man's face immediately before me. It was Sathya Sai Baba of India, and he was smiling, but his eyes were closed. Next, I was aware of his hands lifting me out of my physical body. I experienced a sense of great joy as, at the time, I was very taken by Sai Baba's teachings. Next, I was aware of being stretched as if I were made of elastic. Presently, someone else took the place of Sai Baba. Someone who was genderless and had a wise presence, but showed a cool detachment from me. The 'presence' indicated that he was about to take me to a Russian laboratory.

Next, I was aware of being in a room filled with the sound of whirring machines that looked like computers. There were men standing around, wearing white coats, talking in a foreign language. Suddenly, the machines sounded a warning signal and, almost immediately, I became aware of a copper-colored dome shaped object descending rapidly towards me. The voice of the 'presence' was speaking in my ear, telling me that we had to leave quickly. He later explained that the 'dome' was designed to detect the presence of the astral body and trap it. Apparently, I had been trespassing upon 'top secret' property. I can only think that the 'presence,' which seemed benevolent, had taken me to the laboratory to forewarn me of the danger that existed in the astral world.

Sometime later my boyfriend, who was a computer consultant, described how scientists were designing a metal container which could entrap the astral body. About this time, I came across Robert Monroe's work on astral projection and his own experiences of being in a metal cage that shielded the user against electromagnetic energy. He had discovered that his astral body was unable to pass in or out of the cage. Understandably, I was excited about this piece of information as it validated my personal experiences.

The final experience was richly detailed and very atmospheric. I was aware of having an OBE rather than an ordinary dream.

'There was a presence with me that informed me I was in South America and about to enter a hidden library where details of every person's life and lives were kept. Although I have no memory of the library being subterranean, I do remember it being set in a red sandstone building which could have been a cave. There was a person at the entrance who I believed to be a librarian or record keeper who allowed me to enter and start looking at the books in one area. She explained that I wasn't to take out any of the books to read and that I wasn't ready to process this information. I remember just touching several bound copies and, without having to open the pages, the words seemed to flow into my mind. My stay was brief because the presence was telling me we had to leave and that I would be able to come back some time in the future.'

I believe these were the 'akashic records', which are a cosmic blueprint or DNA of everything that has happened to every human soul and the various incarnations they have had on the earth. The mystic, Alice Bailey, described them through her Tibetan Guide as 'an immense photographic film, registering all the desires and earth experiences of our planet. Those who perceive it will see pictured thereon: The life experiences of every human being since time began, the reactions to the experience of the entire animal kingdom, the aggregation of the thought-forms of a karmic nature (based on desire) of every human unit throughout time.

'When exteriorized, I found myself racing through the air, the wind against my face. I came to a dwelling and passed through the dark wooden panels of the building. The house was unfamiliar; small, rough and uncarpeted. Ahead of me was a kitchen and, next to it, a bedroom. Passing into the bedroom I stood between two beds and gazed through the window onto a beautiful sunset. There were mountains ahead and I remember thinking that I must be in another part of the world as it had been morning when I had left my home in Brighton and there was nothing higher than a hill there. I had a hunch that I was somewhere in South America.

Next, I passed through the walls to a place where I could hear voices. Passing through the door, I saw a group of men dressed in safari-type shirts and neckties playing cards at a table and drinking. They had dark complexions and seemed oblivious of my presence. But, what really drew my attention was a small man sitting with knees drawn up to his chin by the window. He was dressed in a plain white robe, but his features were far from plain. His head was huge, conical and totally out of proportion with the rest of his body. He had no hair on his head and his face was without lines and yellow in color. Unlike the others, he *was* aware of my presence. It was difficult to say whether the men playing cards were aware of him or not. At first, I wondered if he had hydrocephalus and yet, knowing that patients I had seen were unable to support the head, I dismissed this.

It was a strange feeling to see him sitting there, unmoving, his intense blue eyes regarding me silently and sadly...... '

I was unable to shrug off this haunting impression for several days afterwards.

I also wondered if the 'being' would have been interpreted by another observer as an alien intelligence.'

Recently, I met Pam Callow, a Cumbrian lady, who was

kind enough to share several of her experiences with me.

'Thirteen years ago, I was in the Caribbean on a cruise with my daughter. I wasn't awake, yet I wasn't asleep either. I was just conscious... I was aware of being in a beautiful green field with a hill. Next, I was aware of a man with top hat and a city wall made up of big blocks of stone. I remember thinking "Where am I? I'm meant to be on a ship!" My heart began to beat very fast as it always does with these experiences'

About 4-5 years ago, Pam had another experience in mid July. She found herself out in space amidst a mass of stars that went on forever. She described space as being vast, beautiful and very peaceful. It was the vastness and deep silence that she was most struck by.

3 years ago, she had found herself riding on the back of Pegasus. She could hear the swishing of its wings as they flew. She described the softness of its fur and feathers beneath her and remembered thinking; 'How am I going to get home?' She also described seeing a curtain of silver rain in the sky and was left with a fantastic feeling.

She went on to say that she had visited a lot of worlds/planets and on each one, she knew that there was life, but not as we know it. On one planet, she saw a one eyed octopus being and knew that this was the life form that inhabited it.

I want to follow this with Carl Jung's personal and richly detailed description of an OBE/NDE and cover a diversity of compelling experiential insights which are hard to find in many accounts. He has also written it from an observational perspective rather than a merely personal one. The experience is a direct quote from Jung's book, *Memories, Dreams, Reflections,* an experience which seems to correspond to the higher dimensions, which I have mentioned earlier, and can be accessible to the astral traveler.

In 1944, following a heart attack, he lay ill and close to death. Jung admitted that during this period he didn't think he would live very long. His nurse described to him her experience of him: 'It was as if you were surrounded by a bright glow' which was a phenomenon she had often observed in the dying. Jung himself said that he didn't know whether he was dreaming or in a state of near ecstasy. These were the experiences he recorded that are too important in their nature to not be transcribed here. Interestingly, Jung only included this work in his writings later on in life because he was concerned that his scientific stature would crumble.

It seemed to me that I was high up in space. Far below, I saw the globe of the Earth, bathed in a gloriously blue light. I saw the deep blue sea and the continents. Far below my feet, lay Ceylon and, in the distance, ahead of me, the subcontinent of India. My field of vision did not include the whole Earth, but its global shape was plainly distinguishable and its outlines shone with a silvery gleam through that wonderful blue light. In many places the globe seemed colored, or spotted dark green like oxidized silver. Far away to the left lay a broad expanse – the reddish-yellow desert of Arabia; it was as though the silver of the Earth had assumed a reddish-gold hue. Then came the Red Sea, and far, far back – as if in the upper left of a map – I could just make out a bit of the Mediterranean. My gaze was directed chiefly toward that. Everything else appeared indistinct. I could also see the snow-covered Himalayas, but in that direction it was foggy or cloudy. I did not look to the right at all. I knew that I was on the point of departing from the Earth.

Later, I discovered how high in space one would have to be to have so extensive a view – approximately a thousand miles! The sight of the Earth from this height was the most glorious thing I had ever seen.

After contemplating it for a while, I turned around. I had been standing with my back to the Indian Ocean, as it were, and my face to the north. Then it seemed to me that I made a turn to the south. Something new entered my field of vision. A short distance away I saw in space a tremendous dark block of stone, like a meteorite. It was about the size of my house, or even bigger. It was floating in space, and I myself was floating in space.

I had seen similar stones on the coast of the Gulf of Bengal. They were blocks of tawny granite, and some of them had been hollowed out into temples. My stone was one such gigantic dark block. An entrance led into a small antechamber. To the right of the entrance, a black Hindu sat silently in lotus posture upon a stone bench. He wore a white gown, and I knew that he expected me. Two steps led up to this antechamber, and inside, on the left, was the gate to the temple. Innumerable tiny niches, each with a saucer-like concavity filled with coconut oil and small burning wicks, surrounded the door with a wreath of bright flames. I had once actually seen this when I visited the Temple of the Holy Tooth at Kandy in Ceylon; the gate had been framed by several rows of burning oil lamps of this sort.

As I approached the steps leading up to the entrance into the rock, a strange thing happened: I had the feeling that everything was being sloughed away; everything I aimed at or wished for or thought, the whole phantasmagoria of earthly existence, fell away or was stripped from me – an extremely painful process. Nevertheless something remained; it was as if I now carried along with me everything I had ever experienced or done, every-thing that had happened around me. I might also say: it was with me, and I was it. I consisted of all that, so to speak. I consisted of my own history and I felt with great certainty: this is what I am. I am this bundle of what has been and what has been accom-plished.

This experience gave me a feeling of extreme poverty, but at the same time of great fullness. There was no longer anything I wanted or desired. I existed in an objective form; I was what I had been and lived. At first the sense of annihilation predominated, of having been stripped or pillaged; but suddenly that became of no consequence.

Everything seemed to be past; what remained was a "fait accompli", without any reference back to what had been. There was no longer any regret that something had dropped away or been taken away. On the contrary: I had everything that I was, and that was everything.

Something else engaged my attention: as I approached the temple I had the certainty that I was about to enter an illuminated room and would meet there all those people to whom I belong in reality. There I would at last understand — that this too was a certainty – what historical nexus I or my life fitted into. I would know what had been before me, why I had come into being, and where my life was flowing. My life as I lived it had often seemed to me like a story that has no beginning and end. I had the feeling that I was a historical fragment, an excerpt for which the preceding and succeeding text was missing. My life seemed to have been snipped out of a long chain of events, and many questions had remained unanswered. Why had it taken this course? Why had I brought these particular assumptions with me? What had I made of them? What will follow? I felt sure that I would receive an answer to all the questions as soon as I entered the rock temple. There I would meet the people who knew the answer to my question about what had been before and what would come after.

While I was thinking over these matters, something happened that caught my attention. From below, from the direction of Europe, an image floated up. It was my doctor, or rather, his likeness – framed by a golden chain or a golden laurel wreath. I knew at once: 'Aha, this is my doctor, of course, the one who has been treating me. But now he is coming in his primal form. In life

54

he was an avatar of the temporal embodiment of the primal form, which has existed from the beginning. Now he is appearing in that primal form.

Presumably I too was in my primal form, though this was something I did not observe but simply took for granted. As he stood before me, a mute exchange of thought took place between us. The doctor had been delegated by the Earth to deliver a message to me, to tell me that there was a protest against my going away. I had no right to leave the Earth and must return. The moment I heard that, the vision ceased. I was profoundly disappointed, for now it all seemed to have been for nothing. The painful process of defoliation had been in vain, and I was not to be allowed to enter the temple, to join the people in whose company I belonged.

In reality, a good three weeks were still to pass before I could truly make up my mind to live again. I could not eat because all food repelled me. The view of city and mountains from my sickbed seemed to me like a painted curtain with black holes in it, or a tattered sheet of newspaper full of photographs that meant nothing. Disappointed, I thought, 'Now I must return to the "box system" again.' For it seemed to me as if behind the horizon of the cosmos a three-dimensional world had been artificially built up, in which each person sat by himself in a little box. And now I should have to convince myself all over again that this was important! Life and the whole world struck me as a prison, and it bothered me beyond measure that I should again be finding all that quite in order. I had been so glad to shed it all, and now it had come about that I – along with everyone else – would again be hung up in a box by a thread.

I felt violent resistance to my doctor because he had brought me back to life. At the same time, I was worried about him. His life is in danger, for heaven's sake! He has appeared to me in his primal form! When anybody attains this form it means he is going to die, for already he belongs to the "greater company".

Suddenly the terrifying thought came to me that the doctor would have to die in my stead. I tried my best to talk to him about it, but he did not understand me. Then I became angry with him.

In actual fact I was his last patient. On April 4, 1944 – I still remember the exact date I was allowed to sit up on the edge of my bed for the first time since the beginning of my illness, and on this same day the doctor took to his bed and did not leave it again. I heard that he was having intermittent attacks of fever. Soon afterward he died of septicemia. He was a good doctor; there was something of the genius about him. Otherwise he would not have appeared to me as an avatar of the temporal embodiment of the primal form.

There are several elements about this experience which suggest it was both a NDE, OBE *and* a lucid dream, in that Jung retained full awareness throughout. Often in an OBE, content of the experience becomes jumbled and lost. But there was another unique component of the experience, it was prophetic. Jung saw his doctor in his 'primal form' and believed that it presaged death. This came to pass. Above all, this experience was a transpersonal one, in that it moved beyond the realm of the personal and psychic, into the spiritual and esoteric domain. No wonder Jung kept this a secret until his death.

In the next chapter we will look at lucid dreaming.

Chapter 6

Lucid Dreaming

'Row, row, row your boat,
Gently down the stream.
Merrily, merrily, merrily,
Life is but a dream.'
(US Nursery Rhyme,1892)

This well known lyric sung by adults and children worldwide is really a working template for our daily life. As many visionaries and mystics, such as Gurdjieff and Baba Ram Dass have intimated, life is but a dream. Furthermore, they believe that it is our task to wake up to this reality and become conscious. Yet, most of the time we walk around unconscious, believing that all we perceive in this world, particularly prosperity, career and status, is a reality in itself. Accepting this as a reality, we become so attached to this mindset and the illusion of everyday existence that we become imprisoned in a dream castle of our own making. In believing this, we deny ourselves the horizon of infinite possibilities, and become only a shadow of our true potential.

Supposing this life is but a dream and that we only have to wake up to this?

Would we want to wake up? Or would we choose to remain unconscious because it is too terrifying to think or believe it can be any other way?

Yet, we have a growing population of young people who are searching for another reality through drugs. Surely, this would not be so if we lived in a world that not only accepted the possibility of altered states of consciousness taking place spontaneously, but understood that we are ever in the midst of infinite possibility. I am reminded of Wordsworth's compelling lines: 'trailing clouds of glory do we come, from God, who is our home.'

In our modern world, not only do we deny our young this connection with their spiritual birthright, but we instill in them that to believe otherwise is dangerous because it enters into the realm of psychosis and schizophrenia. With no spiritual anchor to harness their dreams, is there any wonder they become addicted to alcohol and drugs?

Until fairly recently, the subject of lucid dreaming has remained in the wings of the scientific world until Stephen Laberge, PhD, studied psychophysiology at Stanford University and became involved in research on lucid dreaming for over a decade. As well as writing several popular books about lucid dreaming, he went on to found the 'Institute of Lucidity' in California. As a result, lucid dreaming has become an accepted science in itself.

One of the salient features of lucid dreaming is the sheer clarity and intensity of impact on the recipient. The dreamer experiences a deep sense of joy and peace that is rare in the ordinary waking state. More than anything, the dreamer knows that they are dreaming. They will think 'I am dreaming this'. The moment this is realized the spell is broken. The dreamer realizes that they can make things happen and control the contents of the dream. In a way, the dreamer becomes their own director; catching hold of scenes and exercising some autonomy over their content.

Amidst the many astral projections in my twenties, one sequence seems to stand out and I'll include it here:

'I was with a small group of people when I realized that I didn't have to walk. I could propel myself across the ground. Enjoying this unexpected source of freedom, I turned somersaults and cartwheels in the air and experienced a sense of euphoria in realizing my new sense of autonomy. I remember thinking it must be like being on the moon with a sixth of the earth's gravity. I enjoyed an expansive sense of freedom and control over my circumstances.

Although, in the dream, I was only in a village hall, everything, the people around me, the quality of light in the room converged together to become a transcendental experience. I remember wanting the dream to go on and on forever...'

If I am to make a distinction between a lucid dream and an OBE, this is discernible in both the symptoms and level of autonomy. Basically, there are no tangible physical symptoms as there are in an OBE such as buzzing, roaring in the ears and possible anxiety at finding yourself outside of your body. Instead, there is a greater sense of autonomy and enjoyment. With an astral projection there may be little control at first for the beginner to exert their will to navigate where they want to go or even to return to the physical body. The only hindrance to retaining full memory of lucid dreaming is in endeavoring to remain conscious so that one doesn't slip back into a normal dream state and possibly forget the whole experience. Lucid dreams occur during Rapid Eye Movement(REM). Because of this, Stephen LaBerge has developed this further by encouraging subjects in his dream laboratory to signal to him through moving their eyes left and right eight times in succession to indicate that they are conscious.

Most waking dreams appear to maintain a pleasurable state of being and are really like having access to an enjoyable recreational tool at the least and, at the most, the possibility of developing one's spiritual consciousness. Also, according to extensive research, lucid dreams are more likely to take place just before waking up. Although stress factors in the life can precipitate a lucid dream, overexcitement can pull one rapidly back to waking consciousness. Emotional stability is the key here.

All researchers in the area of lucid dreaming seem to agree on several ways of preparing for a 'waking dream'. These are asking oneself throughout the day, 'Am I awake or am I dreaming?' It is a lot harder to do than one would expect! This is because consciousness is involved, and how many of us are fully conscious throughout the day? We might think we are, but are we really?

Many of our everyday tasks are repetitive and so we barely need to be conscious to perform them. This same question, 'Am I awake or am I dreaming?' can also be applied to the dreaming state.

The suggested way of 'waking up' in a dream according to both *New Scientist* magazine and Carlos Castaneda, is to focus on one's hands throughout the dreaming episode. By bringing consciousness to a focal part of the body one connects with waking consciousness. But this is notoriously hard to do and like astral projection, takes practice, practice, and practice! Yet, once the dreamer has experienced a 'lucid dream,' the door to the unconscious is opened. The dreamer realizes that they are both the observer and the dreamer. Being aware of one's 'observing self' is the key to being conscious to the experience, as is writing down the dream material. Committing the lucid dream to paper, earths the psychic material, making it real. Dreams can be like working one's way through glue! They do not want to be captured and made conscious. So to recap on the prerequisites for a lucid dream:

Ask oneself often throughout the day: Am I dreaming?

Concentrate on the hands while in the dream state. And keep up the question: is this a dream?

Keep pen and paper by the bedside and write down the dream immediately before it slips away.

One of the great pioneers in the art of lucid dreaming was Carlos Castaneda who wrote twelve books on shamanism. The first of these was *The Teachings of Don Juan*. In the 1960s, he trained under the tutelage of Yaqui Shaman, Don Juan. Castaneda, an anthropologist, after vanishing from the media for some years, returned in the 1994 with a book called *The Power of Dreaming* which, based on his apprenticeship with Don Juan, explores the art of lucid dreaming by defining the consecutive stages of gaining personal autonomy over one's dreams. These stages are revealed through seven gates of increasing awareness. The first gate is referred to as a 'stabilization' of the dreaming body through becoming aware of seeing one's hands in the dream, then panning out to include other features before returning to the hands. This exercise gives one a centre to return to, a hook to tether the consciousness to. Remember, while experimenting in the area of dreams, it is very hard to resist the drugging and numbing effect of sleep consciousness.

Chapter 7

Preparing for an Astral Projection

Safety is often the first element to be overlooked when wanting to experiment with an OBE. That is why I slot it in here, because personal safety is central to the whole process. When you go to a foreign country you have to have a passport, insurance and an assortment of vaccines that will render you immune to the local viruses. Traveling on the astral planes is no different, although pre-emptive protection is more of a psychic nature.

Similarly, one needs to prepare psychologically for the event, just as you would undergo physical training before tackling a Himalayan expedition. Psychically, there are energy vortices in the body, more commonly known as 'chakras' which need protecting because the astral world is inhabited by many types of beings, both benevolent and others who – well – do not have your best interests at heart and are apt to cause mischief to any beginner on the astral plane. Although, of course, you have your protective guides with you, you cannot expect them to do everything! So avoid any alcohol and especially hallucinogenic substances which could certainly give you an unpleasant run for your money. It is prudent to avoid any mentally or emotionally stimulating films, particularly horror and violence, as these leave a psychic residue in the memory which can and will attract entities you might not want to meet. Also be aware of your emotional state as this will influence your quality of projection. Remember, in the astral world thoughts are literally things and negative emotions like anger and jealousy can attract disturbing experiences.

All these injunctions might seem like a bit of a tall order. Yet, it is no different to applying a health regime to your body if you want to tone up and become fit. In short, a healthy lifestyle cuts out the junk food and includes regular exercise. It goes without saying that the will has to be activated and the mind be focused on the goal of having an out-of -body experience. Just as there are no short cuts to becoming fit or revising for an exam, learning to astral travel has its own safety measures which need to be taken on board. Although there is no terrestrial map to the astral world, there is an internal one of being mindful of what you allow into your consciousness through the media and your thoughts. Like meditation, it isn't something you do spontaneously, it is something you apply your mind and body to and can take a lot of practice. The beginner might be lucky and have a spontaneous projection and, maybe this is what arouses their interest in the first place, but this is not always the case. Additionally, setting some time for meditation or quiet reflection can be harnessed in preparation for the event.

Chances are though that even the most diligent form of preparation and squeaky clean thoughts may not precipitate an astral projection. It might just as easily arise from some trauma or worry that has impacted on your life recently.

A word of warning here, if you have been mentally and emotionally unstable recently, it is ill-advised to practice this, not because it is especially dangerous, but because you need someone around you who knows a little of the map with the ability to discriminate between a genuine psychic experience and psychosis. Sadly, in our modern life, there are too many who pathologize astral projection and, indeed, any psychic experience as schizophrenia or a form of psychosis rather than an experiential adjustment of the psyche. The key here is to realize your own autonomy in the midst of the event, rather than collapse into it.

How to have an astral projection

Although spontaneous projections do occur in about 30 percent of the population, bringing one about consciously takes a lot of practice. All skills, from social to academic or even psychic ones happen 99% of the time as a result of persistence and patience.

If I am to embrace any astral projection theory and technique, I find myself recommending Robert Monroe's work as this is the one I have used in my own practice and, therefore, has been an intrinsic part of my experience.

There are several prerequisites or rules for an astral projection to take place and these are:

- Ensure that you won't be disturbed. Mobile phones and landlines need to be switched off and unplugged.
- If possible, let the people who share the house with you know that you are not to be disturbed.
- If you have animals, make sure they won't disturb you. Animals are particularly receptive to psychic influences and may want to be near you during your practice. (I had a cat that used to sit near my face when I was astral projecting which on one level could be reassuring, but on another could evoke fears of being suffocated!)
- Make your body as comfortable as possible on a bed or settee and wear loose clothing.
- Take care to ensure that the room temperature is comfortable. If you are too hot, you may experience feelings of suffocation. Similarly, if you are too cold,

it is hard to focus your mind.

- Assume a bodily position conducive to astral projection. Usually this is lying on your back with your hands at your side. I have found this position to be conducive to exteriorization. (Often, after returning to my physical body, I have awoken to find my arms crossed over my chest. Although I have never assumed this position consciously, I have come to understand that this is a protective position that is often adopted by people who astral project regularly. Even if I go to sleep on my side, after waking up in my body, I have found that my body has always assumed this protective position.)

- The next stage is controlling your breathing by taking long easy breaths and exhaling slowly. Don't strain to do this. Do it comfortably. As you breathe, relax the muscles in your body, moving from the toes upwards. Lastly, relax your facial muscles, paying special attention to the throat and ensuring your jaw is relaxed, mouth slightly open.

You may have to practice this a few times before reaching the right level of relaxation. Scenes of the waves rolling up and down the beach can be very helpful and fall in with the rhythm of your breathing.

After some time and effort you will experience a 'hum' or 'buzz' in your head which will become weaker or stronger according to the level of your consciousness. The stronger or louder it is, the closer you are to 'lift off'! The temptation here is to become excited and blow the whole thing, because excitement jolts one into full waking consciousness. Try to accept the buzzing, humming and temporary somatic paralysis. Allow these sensations to wash over you in waves. Be aware that you have entered an initial threshold and just relax deeper, rather than getting excited about it. Immediate emotions have a direct bearing on the quality of the transition. Expect a bit of a rocky ride at first as the 'hum'or 'buzz', which can sometimes be a 'roar', rocks you about. This is an energetic transitional state of being and rarely happens smoothly without practice. It is a bit like riding a scooter for the first time when there is some kangaroo jumping around until you gain mastery of the throttle. It is the same with OBEs. The rocking about sensation is the astral body attempting to disengage with the physical body. Normally it would just exteriorize, no problems. But once the driver is conscious and wants to take control, that's when the problem begins. Control comes later after a good deal of practice. If you practice meditation or deep relaxation on a regular basis, then you are halfway there!

As experience comes into play, you will begin to realize that when your 'observing self' becomes agitated or excited, this causes the rocky ride because instincts are pulling against a natural process.

Another disturbing stage you need to prepare yourself for is a temporary sense of paralysis which can be uncomfortable and frightening until you realize that this is a natural part of the process too.

Having experienced this many times myself, I understand what primal feelings this can evoke. In my teens, when I experienced OBE's on a regular basis, I compromised my ability to 'lift out' many times by becoming consumed by fear.

Since our early memories of the birth experience, although largely unconscious, can evoke feelings of suffocation and leaving a safe haven, this early experience can be compared with a similar transitional state of 'birthing' one's astral body into full awareness.

Sleep paralysis, although quite normal, is a necessary safety mechanism to prevent us acting out our dreams in the form of sleepwalking. Although this affects voluntary motor activities, it does not affect involuntary activities like breathing, circulation and eye movement. Rather than being afraid of this brief transitional state, I have come to look upon it as a necessary safety belt to prevent me harming myself. After all, it would be even worse if, I were to run downstairs in my dream and woke up in hospital after suffering concussion as a result. Sadly, these things do happen if sleep paralysis does not take place.

As time in the astral world does not correspond to our understanding of time in everyday life, any uncomfortable moments, because they are so subjective, can appear to be interminable. Similarly, euphoric experiences are lingering and help moor our soul to a heightened state of consciousness.

At some point the fluctuating hum or buzz in the head which proceeds projection, becomes 'less rough', as Monroe defines it, and more even.

The sound which can be a roar in the head fluctuates less in response to feelings of excitement or panic and there is a steady purr like that of a motorbike or lawn mower. It is this 'edge' that maintains the liminal state between waking and sleeping. If the roar begins to fade, bring the sound back again or you may fall asleep and remember nothing of what has happened before. Liminal states hold great power, reminding me of something I read many years ago in Carlos Castaneda's writings where his teacher, Don Juan, revealed that the greatest power lay in the liminal state, for example twilight, which was referred to as the 'gap between two worlds.' In this place of betwixt and between lies the greatest potential, reminiscent of what the Tibetans refer to as the 'bardo', a stage between life and death, between lifetimes.

When the humming/buzzing has stabilized to an even keel, you are ready to leave your physical body and do not have to make an effort to do this. It usually just happens. Again, excitement can affect the quality of the experience; for example you may be absolutely exhilarated to find yourself whizzing through the air, passing through walls and ceilings as if they were not there. Or there may be the fear of banging your head on the ceiling and the shock can suddenly cause you to interiorize.

At first, there is no control over where you are going or who you are going to meet. But don't worry about this. Control will come in its own time as you become more experienced and confidence grows. Until then it's rather like being let loose on a pair of roller skates or ferrying along on a surf board or hang glider.

Remember though, you are never alone. There is always a guide with you or your helper. Endeavoring to remember this will create a gateway of communication between your guide and yourself. Although words may not be exchanged, their guiding presence will be tangible.

As time passes and you become more accustomed to the astral world, you will be able to gain greater autonomy over your astral state. You can travel at the speed of thought, watching the territory fly beneath you as you proceed towards a destination already visualized in your head.

And do remember, when you awaken, to jot down your experience in that notebook!

Although astral journeying may appear to be very lucid and memorable at the time, once you awaken in normal everyday consciousness, it is surprising how quickly the mundane world eclipses the memory. Remember also, that most people have OBEs but there are very few who have awareness of this in their everyday life—just because they dismissed their experiences as mere dreams and didn't bother taking notes. If you invest in your unconscious world, the more it will invest in you by becoming conscious. After all, without diligent note-taking, Jung, one of our greatest psychiatrists whose work on dreams was outstanding, would never have contributed to our understanding of the unconscious. I believe, although he never said as much, he was a pioneer in astral projection.

Bibliography and Further Reading

Castaneda, Carlos, *The Art of Dreaming*, Element Books, an imprint of HarperCollins, 2004

Godwin, Malcolm, *The Lucid Dreamer*, Element Books, 1995

Green, Celia, *Out-Of-The-Body Experiences*, The Institute of Psychophysical Research, 1977

Jung, Carl, Memories, Dreams, Reflections, Fontana paperbacks, 1983

Marlarkey, Kevin and Alex, *The boy who came back from heaven* Tyndale House publishers, 2007.

Monroe, Robert, *Journeys Out-Of-The-Body*, Doubleday, 1971

Muldoon and Carrington, *The Projection of the Astral Body*, Kessinger Publishing, 2010

Nelson, Kevin, New Scientist, 22 December 2010

Ritchie, George, *Return from Tomorrow*, Reville Books, 1978

Snell, Joy, *The Ministry of Angels: Here and Beyond*, Kessinger Publishing, 2006

Useful Websites

www.monroeinstitute.org/

www.lucidipedia.com/blog/2011/04/30/stephen-laberge-per...

www.arthurfindlaycollege.org/2012all.html

Stephaniesorrell.com

6th Books investigates the paranormal, supernatural, explainable or unexplainable. Titles cover everything included within parapsychology: how to, lifestyles, beliefs, myths, theories and memoir.